seventeen

presents...

traumarama!

Real girls share their most embarrassing moments ever!

seventeen
presents...

traumarama!

Real girls share their most embarrassing moments ever!

From the Editors of Seventeen Magazine

Illustrations by Megan Hess

Hearst Books
A Division of Sterling Publishing Co., Inc.
New York

Copyright © 2005 by Hearst Communications, Inc.

Library of Congress Cataloging-in-Publication Data

Seventeen magazine's traumarama! : real girls share their
most embarrassing moments ever / from the editors of
Seventeen magazine.
Includes index.
    p. cm.
 ISBN 1-58816-517-5
 1. Teenage girls--United States--Attitudes. 2.
Embarrassment. I. Seventeen magazine.
  HQ798.S448 2005
  305.235'2'0973--dc22
                       2005013113

10 9 8 7 6 5 4 3 2

www.seventeen.com

For information about custom editions, special sales,
premium and corporate purchases, please contact Sterling
Special Sales Department at 800-805-5489 or
specialsales@sterlingpub.com

Distributed in Canada by Sterling Publishing
c/o Canadian Manda Group, 165 Dufferin Street
Toronto, Ontario, Canada M6K 3H6

Distributed in Australia by Capricorn Link (Australia)
Pty. Ltd. P.O. Box 704, Windsor, NSW 2756 Australia
Printed in China

Sterling ISBN-13: 978-1-58816-517-6
      ISBN-10: 1-58816-517-5

Dressing Rooms

see page 224

see page 28

Happy New Year

see page 31

see page 120

contents

Check Point

see page 221

see page 218

see page 221

see page 34

You're not the only one to completely humiliate yourself, sister

My friends are always saying stuff to me like, "I can't believe you just *said* that!" or "You are **insane** for printing that horrible picture of yourself in **Seventeen**!" As far as they're concerned, I'm like a walking, talking **embarrassing** moment. But the thing is, *I'm* never really embarrassed by **any** of it. If anything, I *look* for moments with ultimate humiliation potential and willingly (with great pleasure!) dive right into them. I know, I know—you probably think I need to be **institutionalized,** but hear me out.

This is how I see it: I'm genuinely comfortable with who I am. Like, I know I'm not an idiot because I work really hard every day, and I'm always looking to learn from other people. I know I'm not ugly because I truly **believe** that everyone in the world is beautiful (including you!), so that, of course, extends to me as well. And I know I'm not a bad person because any time I do something that feels uncomfortable to me morally (because let's face it, no one is **perfect**), I work as hard as I can to fix things so I can feel good about myself again.

So basically I've got **nothing** to hide, and I guess that's why I have no shame. Listen, I'm not necessarily saying that's a *good* thing (my mom probably thinks a little shame would do me good!), but it certainly makes me a funny girl to be around. I'll do **anything** for a laugh, and I guess this book is proof of that. It's the first book I've ever been a part of, and my **friends** would say it makes perfect sense that it's a collection of humiliating moments: my favorite kind! So I hope you enjoy the stories. And the next time you find yourself in one of those moments? Think of me and lean into it, sister! If you laugh at **yourself,** the rest of the world will be laughing *with* you (and not *at* you!).

I continue to **adore** you, and I am so grateful for all the support you show me and the magazine! You know where I am if you ever **need** me (or just want to share your most mortifying moment!)—
atoosa@seventeen.com.

"as we
started
to make out...
I farted!"

see page 21

guys

The most extreme embarrassment: IFOC (in front of crush).

control freak

"It was my first day as a lifeguard, and the **cute** supervisor showed me the theme park's control room. As he checked the pressure of the wave machine, his face went pale. "The whole place is going to **explode**!" he said. I ran for the exit; he grabbed the door handle first. It was stuck! I started **screaming**—until he laughed. Nothing was wrong, but he said it was the best joke he'd ever played on anyone!"

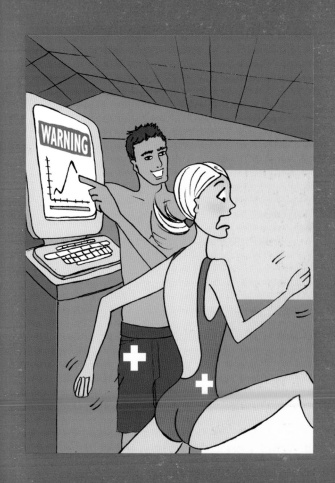

lip schtick

" I was riding the bus with my boyfriend, and he said something really sweet, so I started **smiling.** He looked at me and asked if I'd put on **lipstick** that morning. I thought it was because he thought I looked cute. But then he said I had a lot of red **gunk** on my two front teeth. I was sort of horrified! "

can it!

"

Okay, so I was at our town's big beach party, and I spotted the guy I like. My friends kept telling me to go talk to him, so I did. He was sitting by an open **cooler** that I figured was for everybody, so I reached in, grabbed a soda, and sat next to him. There was an **awkward** silence, so I opened the can and offered him some. He said no and looked at me even weirder. That's when I realized what I'd done. I'd been so nervous going up to him that I hadn't even looked at what I'd grabbed—it was one of his dad's **beers**! I felt so dumb!

"

bread and shudder

"I was dining in the food court with a bunch of friends and my crush. Unfortunately, I had a **cold sore** the size of Everest at the corner of my **mouth**. When I was in the middle of eating my sandwich, my crush tactfully informed me that there was a piece of **bread** on my lip. As everyone at the table unsuccessfully attempted to muffle their laughter, he leaned over to brush away the "crumb." Well, despite the high **yuck** factor of that moment, we've been dating ever since.

potato head

> I work with my friend at the local fast-food place, where we often **goof** around to pass the time. Once, while stationed at the drive-through, I thought it would be funny to stick french **fries** in my **nose** before leaning out to take orders. Of course, the next person in line was the **hottest** guy at our school.

red-faced

"

At a school dance, I was making out with a guy in a closet. The kiss felt really **wet,** but I didn't want to stop. Finally he pulled away, pointed at my face and said, "What's that?" I touched my cheek, and before I could figure out what was wrong he said, "You're **bleeding**!" I'd gotten a nosebleed, mid-makeout! The blood was all over both of our faces. Guess he was **grossed out,** because he rushed out of the closet and left me standing there.

"

silent but deadly

" I went to a club with some of my girlfriends, and we **hooked** up with a couple of guys we knew. After we'd been dancing for an hour, we needed to take a little **rest**. The guy I was with sat down and I sat on his lap. Just as we started to make out...i **farted**! It was a real warm one too! It was terrible. He awkwardly said he needed to use the bathroom—but he **never** came back. "

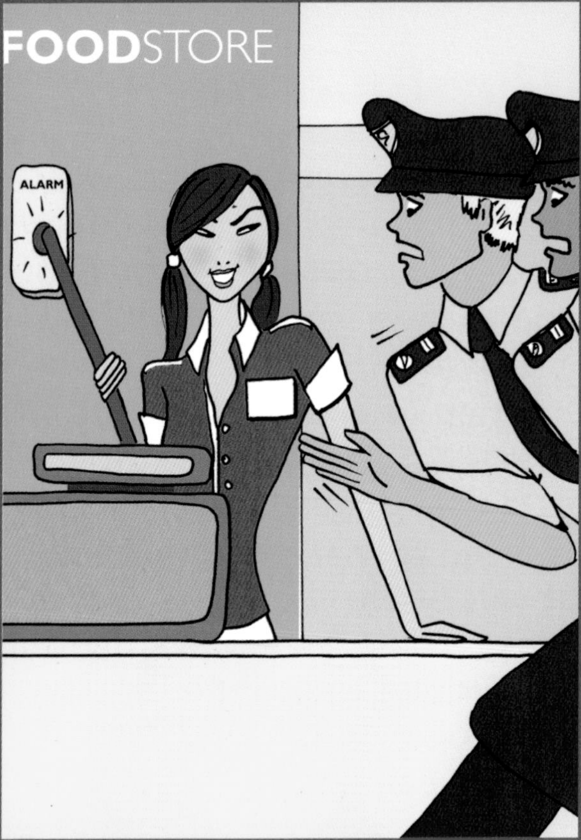
FOODSTORE
ALARM

alarming incident

"I was cleaning up in the convenience store where I work when a group of policemen pulled up. I figured that they'd come to buy **coffee,** so I didn't think twice about it. As they **rushed** in, I greeted them flirtatiously (a few were really cute). They just stood there and looked at me oddly. It turned out that I had accidentally pushed the **emergency** button, and they had hurried over because they thought the store was being held up!"

guys

fry guy

"Boy, was I wrong in thinking that my fast-food **career** would improve when we got a good-looking new manager. While I was making some fries, he came up behind me to ask me out. **Surprised** by the sound of his voice and that he was interested in me, I quickly swung around while holding the basket—and dripped **scalding** grease on his hand. Not only did I lose the guy, but I nearly lost my *job*."

guys

tall tales

"I was sitting in the cafeteria with my friends when I decided to play a little **joke** on them. They all knew I was totally in love with this guy Brian, so I decided to tell them I was **dating** him. They stared at me in shock as I told them how he had called and said he loved me. The tale was really getting good when I heard a **voice** behind me say, "So, when did all this happen?" I turned around and there was Brian!"

cold call

"For more than two months I'd been crushing on this guy. When I finally got his **number,** I began anonymously calling him from the pay phone down the street, just to hear his voice. The fourth time I called, I spoke up—but in a **disguised** voice. I said "Hi, I really like you." He asked if I was in any of his **classes**. When I answered, "Yeah, two," he said, "This is Sadie, isn't it?" He **knew**! I hung up immediately."

hairy situation

"For my birthday, my friend invited us over to go in her **hot tub**. I wanted to look my best and didn't plan on putting my head under water, so I decided to try a hair **extension**. But at the party a guy playfully dunked me. I checked my head after I came back up but didn't notice any problems—until my friend turned off the jets, and one of the guys pulled my fake hair out of the **filter**! He held it up in front of everyone, and I shamefully had to claim it."

burning love

"

My best friend was throwing a huge **soirée** and the hot guy I'd been corresponding with online was going to be there. Right before midnight, we'd all gone outside to light **sparklers**. As the countdown ended, I turned to give my crush a smooch and bumped into my friend's sparkler—**singeing** my eyebrow. The sparks were definitely flying, but not in the way that I had planned.

"

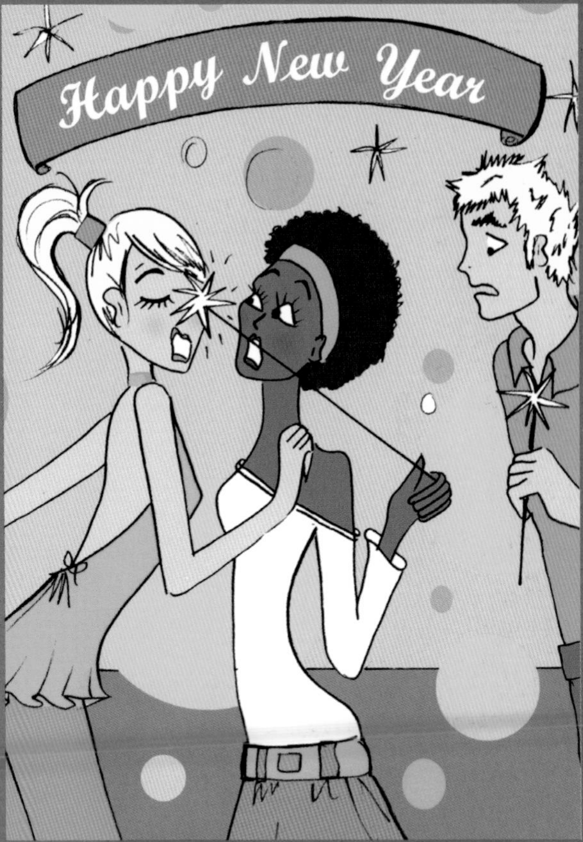
Happy New Year

mouthing off

"My crush and I were sneaking mints in health class while our teacher **droned** on about sex. I wasn't really paying attention to what she was saying, **until** she suddenly said "blow job"! Three spit-drenched candies **flew** out of my mouth and onto my crush's **shirt.** Now he pretty much stays five feet away whenever we talk!"

trick question

"The Valentine's dance was coming up, so I was excited when this guy I liked wanted to meet me after school right after the bell rang to ask me a **question**. "I just want to know if..." he said, before I cut him off. "Yes I'll go to the dance with you," I blurted out, **kissing** him on the cheek. Then, the horror: "Actually could you ask **Jessica** if she wants to go with me?""

southern exposure

"I was in the airport of this small town, where only a few planes leave each day. The airport is totally **tiny**, so it only has one bathroom for everyone to use. I went in, and while I was sitting there doing my business, the door **flew** open and this guy who looked about two years older than me was standing in the doorway. At a loss for words, I just sort of blurted out, "Someone's in here!" The guy totally **froze** while I was sitting there with my pants down to the ground!"

heated conversation

" While chatting with this **gorgeous** babe at a backyard party, I decided to lean seductively on a table. I didn't realize that the **"table"** was actually a burning **grill**. "

faux pas

" It was my very first Valentine's Day with a serious boyfriend. We went out for dinner, and he draped a **beautiful** gold necklace on me. I was so flattered—until later that night, when I noticed a gross **green** ring around my neck! My guy swore the jewelry was real, but his friend told me he'd **found** the necklace on the street and just picked it up off the *ground*. "

brace yourself

" My friends and I were ostensibly eating chocolate mousse at a fancy restaurant, but really we were **giggling** and staring at the cute waiter. When he finally talked to us, I smiled—and he walked off. I turned toward my friends, and they **gagged**! I had goopy chocolate stuck between my braces. So much for kissing the hot guy— I locked lips with my **toothbrush** instead. "

touch of glass

"One night, while I was **vacationing** with my best friend and her family, her little brother woke up crying. Since her parents had gone for a walk, I went out on the **balcony** in my pj's to try to yell for them—and spotted two major hotties. We were totally checking each other out! I turned around to get my friend from inside, but instead walked **smack** into the glass door she had just closed. I looked back to find the guys in complete hysterics."

neighborhood watch

"While riding around in my new set of wheels, I drove by my **crush's** house, hoping he'd be outside—I wanted to show off my car. I was **psyched** when I saw him in his driveway washing his car. His ripped T-shirt accentuated his nice physique, and believe me, I noticed! He looked so good, I sort of stopped paying **attention** to the road...and hit his curbside mailbox. He came over and asked me, "Are you **drunk**?" So much for a good impression."

chill factor

" Some guy friends were hanging out at my place **playing** some video games when one of them casually asked, "Dude, is it **chilly** in here?" Then there was dead silence, and I realized everyone was **looking** at me. Yipes! I looked down and... my nipples were **playing** pop-up! I ran to the dresser and grabbed a sweater. "

streamline

"

During a school field trip to a national park, my crush stopped to stare out across a **beautiful** brook. I figured now was my chance to make a move, and I walked over to start a conversation. To my **surprise,** he was taking a whiz in the water instead of taking in the view! My cheeks still turn **red** thinking about it.

"

red as a rose

" Last Valentine's Day, anyone at school could purchase a chocolate **rose** and have it sent to someone special. I got one from Steven, my crush of two years. The card said, "LeAnn, I've liked you for so long, and it's about time I did something about it. I love you." After school I walked up to him and gave him a big **kiss.** He looked at me and said, "What are you *doing*?" Turns out my friends had sent me the rose as a **joke.** It was so humiliating. "

47

a cover up

"I was expecting my best friend to stop by, so I left the door to my house unlocked. As I was finishing my shower, the **doorbell** rang and I yelled "come upstairs." After quickly drying off, I walked into my bedroom wearing just a **towel** to find the neighborhood skater guys sitting on my bed. Apparently the **guy** I had always wanted to hang out with had decided to come over to say hello.

gender bender

" When my sister invited me to the mall with her, I ran gel through my new short, spiky 'do, and threw on an old T-shirt and jeans—I don't like **dressing** up. Since the school dance was a week away, we were on a mission to pick up a few last-minute items. My sis found a tie in the same color as her **dress** that she thought her date could wear. She asked the guy working at the register if he liked the tie. "I do," he answered. Then he pointed at me: "But what does **he** think?" "

belly flop

"While keeping an eye on my younger sis at the community pool, I happened to notice a **sexy** swimmer doing flips off the diving platform. I almost passed out when he actually came over to talk to me. But even more surprising was that he spoke to me in **Polish,** which, coincidentally, I know. He was wondering if the girl I was watching was my sister, but I was so flustered that I responded, in Polish, "Yes, my **daughter.**" One look at his terrified expression and my major mistake dawned on me. Needless to say, he didn't hang around."

holy moly

"There's a three-story school attached to my church, and there's an **elevator** inside. Last year my boyfriend and I got **bored** during a church service, so we sneaked into the elevator to make out. It was getting pretty steamy when the doors **opened.** Standing there was my pastor with some **members** of the congregation. For a long time I was scared to even go back to church!"

out of order

"At my last *away* swim meet, I got my **period** in between events. I rushed into the locker room looking for a tampon dispenser but couldn't find one! I was so ticked off. "Where's the **stupid** tampon machine?" I yelled. A moment later, two guys came out of the shower with weird looks on their faces. **Yikes**—wrong locker room."

guys

safety first

"Last year was the first Valentine's Day I had a boyfriend. That morning, my guy surprised me with chocolates and two dozen **roses.** After I was done swooning, I gave him his gift. When he opened it, his face turned **pale.** "I don't think I'm ready for this yet!" he stuttered. I asked him what was **wrong**—I'd only gotten him sunglasses. He opened—a big box of condoms! I found out later that a friend had **played** a prank on me, and replaced the real gift with the condoms!"

a real no-no

"At our huge school formal, I was waiting for someone to ask me to **dance** during a slow song. I saw this guy who I knew liked me, but who I really didn't like (he's a **creep**) walking toward me. He was about to open his mouth and I said, "I know what you're going to ask me, and the answer, is **no.**" He said, "Fine, jeez, I'll tell Kevin you said no." Kevin was a guy I really liked! If only I'd known he told the **jerk** to ask me if I'd dance with him!"

guys

toot, toot!

Atoosa's trauma

" I was hanging out in my dorm room with this guy I'd had a super **crazy** crush on for the past few semesters. It was one of those moments where I was like 'I can't believe he's actually in my room!' He was sitting on my bed, checking out my CDs and I thought I'd be **super** cute and just plop myself next to him. Except when I hopped on the bed, I totally laid a **fart**! We had this total moment where we were both staring at each other with a look of **alarm,** like 'Did that just really happen??' So he forced himself to lay one too and said, "See? We're even!" I know—he couldn't have been **cooler** about it—but I mean...did it have to happen? PS: That was the last time I hung out with him. "

Mild mannered editor by day...

But she lays one devil of a fart!

"My dad got on all fours and followed us through the mall—barking like a crazy dog..."

see page 80

family

Why do our **relatives** always seem to **mortify** the ones they love?

lip service

"It was raining, so my mom gave me a ride to school. As I walked to **class,** I realized I was getting some **weird** looks from people I didn't even know. It wasn't until I went to the **bathroom** that I realized what was up. When I looked in the mirror, I saw my mom had left a big burgundy **lipstick** mark right on my forehead! I was beyond embarrassed!"

family
stink tank

"I had been dating this guy for about a month when my parents decided to have him over for dinner. Things were going really well, until my stomach started to **hurt.** I went to the upstairs bathroom, but just as I was flushing, I heard voices down the hall. My parents were giving my boyfriend a **tour** of the house! I tried to distract them but my parents were intent on showing him the **bathroom.** They opened the door and all filed in...and it totally **stunk**!"

door jam

" My dad and I stopped at a gas station because I **really** had to go! I ran in and did my thing, but when I went to leave, the door wouldn't **budge**. I pounded on the stupid thing, yelling for about 10 minutes before I turned and saw **another** door. I had been banging on the janitor's closet! "

cart blanche

"I was at a hardware store with my mom and went to get her a **cart.** So I walked a few rows and took the first empty one I saw. But while pushing it back, I heard an **announcement** that an elderly lady had lost her cart and her walking cane. I looked in my cart, and there was the **cane**! I was too embarrassed to say anything, so I just ditched the cart immediately."

bare-naked lady

" I threw a summer party and invited my closest friends to camp in my **backyard.** As the night went on, one of my melodramatic friends got freaked out and started talking about **spirits** from beyond. Me and my gullible pals got scared and scurried into the house. When we went in my mom's room to wake her, we found her sprawled on the bed, completely **naked**! My friends still haven't let me live it down. "

awkward pause

" My friend brought a porno video to school and asked if I wanted to take it **home.** I was curious, so I did. When I got home, I put it on—because I wanted to know what a porno is like. My sister and her friend were upstairs hanging out, and suddenly I heard them coming down, so I tried to stop the tape, but hit **pause** instead—just as my **mom** also walked in! They all saw a frozen image of three people having a great time. I was mortified, and the whole ordeal ended with the longest and most embarrassing sex **talk** ever. "

mass confusion

" When I went home for Easter last year, I took my **boyfriend** to meet my parents. The morning we arrived, the whole family walked to Sunday Mass. I **guess** the combination of the heat, the anxiety of the meeting, and the stuffiness of the church got to me, and I passed out right there in the **pew**! The worst part is, the paramedics came and started asking questions and, in front of my parents, who had known my boyfriend for all of five minutes, they asked if I could be **pregnant**! His relationship with my parents got off to an interesting start! "

laying in wait

" I was going to take my boyfriend out for his birthday, so I went to his **house** to pick him up. His mom said he'd be home soon and I could wait in his room. I decided that it would be **hilarious** for him to walk in and find me lying on his bed with a rose in my **mouth**. I waited like that for a few minutes, and when the door opened, I said in a husky voice, "I've been **waiting** for you, baby." And in walks his mom, holding clean laundry! "

second helping

" Me and my mom went to a café. At the counter there was this little sampler plate with bread broken up into pieces. So my mom and I took a piece and then we both took more. Everyone was looking at us like we were crazy, but I ignored them. When we were sitting, I saw a man go up with a used dish and set it down right next to the "sampler plate" then I noticed that there was a sign above it that said, "Please place used plates here." My mom and I had been eating someone's old food! "

shaping up

"My parents put an ad in the paper for this **pool** table we wanted to sell. This one lady called and asked, "What's its **shape**?" I thought it was a pretty silly question to ask, since all pool tables are pretty much the same, but she wanted to know, so I said, "Um, it's just a **rectangle.**" The lady started laughing and said, "No, I mean, what condition is it in?" I was so totally **embarrassed,** I just handed the phone to my mom without saying another word."

rocky horror

"My sister and I were **driving** during a blizzard and our car got stuck in the snow. We didn't know what to do, but a guy came to help. He said to get in the car and **rock** it back and forth while he pushed the car out. We got inside and started **rocking.** After a few minutes, the guy banged on the window and yelled, "When I said rock, I meant put the car in **drive** and then reverse, not to rock *yourselves*." We felt like total idiots!"

wake-up call

"I was baby-sitting my cousin, who's five, when I got my **period**—it was only my third time. I wasn't used to female products yet, and I should have changed my "equipment" before I napped. I **leaked** through my pants, and when my cousin **got up** (before me) she saw the blood and was scared. So she called 911! Paramedics burst in, while my cousin kept yelling, "You're **bleeding**!" I had to explain to everyone that I had only experienced period leakage."

pooh-pooh

" The mall is the biggest hangout in town—you run into everyone. My parents and I were there browsing in the Disney Store when my dad got a bit silly. Just for fun, he broke into Tigger's song-and-dance routine from *Winnie-the-Pooh!* To make matters more horrifying, when my stepmom and I tried to leave the store without him, Dad got on all fours and followed us through the mall barking like a crazy dog. "

oral fixation

"

The dental assistants at my orthodontist's office always wore bubblegum—or grape—**flavored** gloves to make appointments more palatable. But after my first few visits, the hygienists seemed **hesitant** to put their hands in my mouth. One finally asked to see my parents—**alone.** Apparently the staff was annoyed with my unconscious habit of licking their **fingers.** I felt like such a fool!

"

panty line

" So I was shopping with my mom and I started flirting with this **hot guy** at the checkout counter. Everything was fine until my mom came up and said, "We should go back and look at some **undies.**" I gave her a confused look to make her go away, but then she said, "Don't you remember you **messed** up a few old ones last month?" I didn't know what to say, so I just grabbed my mom and left the counter—fast. "

false alarm

"I woke up and headed for the shower. As I turned on the water, I heard the fire **alarm,** so I grabbed my towel and ran out of the bathroom. My dad was standing in the hall **yelling** for me and my **brothers** to go outside. When we got to the yard, my mom was standing there with a camera in her hand. My parents laughed and shouted, "Happy April Fools' Day!" My oldest brother, still confused, ran around saying, "We've got to get the **pets**!" I'm so glad our neighbors didn't see us."

family

berry embarrassing

"   Our neighbors came over to celebrate Thanksgiving with my family and brought home-made cranberry sauce. Things were **hectic,** so my mother told them to put the bowl down on a chair until she could make **room** for it. When the food was finally served, I took my seat. Too bad the bowl of cranberry sauce had the seat first! I **sprang** up and looked down at my chair just when the neighbor asked, "Where's the cranberry sauce I brought?" It was on my **butt,** that's where! "

family
art show

" I had just started taking birth control pills and I didn't want my mom to find out, so I kept my pills in a **box** with my supplies for art class. One night we had some family friends over for dinner, and my mom, who is really **proud** of my art, wanted to show off what I had been working on. I tried to stop her and act as if I was embarrassed, but she **grabbed** my art box off the kitchen counter, and it spilled **open**—my drawings, art supplies, *and* birth control pills scattered all over the place! "

it's all relative

"Days spent at the pool with my friends are always devoted to boy hunting. But this time—for a change—the guys we were **eyeing** actually started talking to us. The hottest of the bunch, who eventually asked me out, looked vaguely **familiar,** but I couldn't quite put my finger on it. Later in the week, he came over to pick me up for our date and do the "meet the **family**" routine. The minute my parents saw him, they started laughing hysterically. Turns out we're distant cousins! Needless to say, we decided to be just **friends.**"

family
birthday suit

" My parents **refused** to throw me a party for my 16th birthday because of my low grades—so my best bud invited me over instead. On the way home, I realized that I had drunk too much soda—I needed the bathroom **desperately**! When we reached my house, I rushed for the bathroom, tugging down my pants as I flicked on the lights. Just then all of my family and friends **jumped** out and yelled, "Surprise!" I zipped up my pants and excused myself. I have never been so **humiliated** in my life! "

family

shop talk

"Gram and Gramps dragged me to the mall to buy me a summer wardrobe. At one store, I chose some things to try on and had to **wait** 10 minutes for a dressing room! I finally went in and tried on a pair of shorts. As I was admiring myself in the mirror, my grandma yelled at the top of her lungs, "Honey, how's the **crotch**?" I heard people snickering online outside, and I could feel my face getting hot. To make matters worse, she made me come out so she could see the **shorts** on me."

family

young love

" We were having a family reunion one Christmas with the extended family. One of my guy cousins had brought a really **fine** friend. I told him I was 14 (which I am, although I'm kind of **short** for my age). He was slightly older. One of my distant relatives came in wearing a **Santa** suit, and while he was giving out presents to the kids, he mistook me for one of my much younger **cousins**! The cute guy assumed I had lied about my age and slowly made his way to the other side of the room. "

potty mouth

" My mom and I were shopping when we made a quick pit stop in a deserted restroom. I was buttoning my pants when my mom **blew** the bottom out of the toilet in the stall next to me. "Good Lord, Mom, that's disgusting!" I said. I opened my stall door and saw my mother standing by the **sink,** laughing—and this huge woman coming out of the Stall of **Doom**! Let's just say: lesson learned. "

checked out

"People tell me I look a lot **older** than I really am. A few years ago, I was at the store with my mom and little **brother,** and the guy at the cash register was **staring** at me. My mother spotted this and said to him (I swear), "For your information, she's 13 years old and way out of your **league.** Stop looking at her as if she were a Victoria's Secret model!" I wanted to run right out of the store."

family

photo finish

"After researching a science project, I was waiting in the **library** for my mother to pick me up. While browsing the shelves, I found a sex-ed book and made copies of the male form as a **joke** for a few of my friends. Six pictures later the librarian coldly informed me that **copies** cost a dime apiece. I didn't have any money, so when Mom came, the librarian handed her the pix and **demanded** 60 cents! I was grounded— one week for each copy."

hand-delivered

> My boyfriend and I were in my **room** talking about school stuff when I heard **footsteps** coming up the stairs. The door opened, and it was my mom. She said, "here—I picked these up for you"—and threw a **giant** box of **tampons** to me.

shower power

"I was trying to persuade my nephew to take a bath. Finally I convinced him to run the water while we played a game in the hallway. It was taking an awfully long time for the tub to fill, so I checked and discovered that he'd tricked me by not plugging the drain. I pressed a button on the faucet to plug the drain, but the shower came on instead and I got drenched! When his parents arrived moments later, I was the only one who'd had a bath."

full moon

" I had a guy pal over and we were about to go swimming in my **backyard** pool. But my mom was lying there **sunbathing**—in her thong bikini! As if that wasn't bad *enough*, she actually had the nerve to ask me to rub **suntan** oil on her butt! "

family

close call

" I was dancing very close with my date during the last **song** of the night. My mom was scheduled to pick us up, but she arrived a little **early.** Instead of just waiting in the car like a normal person, she actually came into the gym, marched **straight** over to us and told my guy to take a **step** back. She had him put an arm's length between us and said, "*This* is the way you dance with my daughter!" "

family

off his rocker

"My family and I had gone to one of my mom's colleague's houses for a dinner **party.** I was on my best behavior because my mom is super strict about us being very proper in front of other people. To make her proud, I was trying to be really **helpful.** So when this one family arrived and said they'd never been to this person's house before, I **offered** to give them a tour (after all, I'd been there zillions of times with my mom). During the tour, I dramatically pushed open the door to the downstairs **bathroom** and said, "And here's the most important room in the house!" And that's when we saw my mom's **boss** jump up from the toilet, with his pants and boxers around his ankles, to push the door back shut! I never saw a man move that fast and I **never** made eye contact with him again!"

"I had no choice but to wipe my butt with her towel..."

see page 121

friends

It's so **true** what they always say: humiliation loves **company**.

friends

bull's eye

"One birthday I got together with some friends. A group of them were playing **darts,** and I absent-mindedly wandered near the dartboard. A guy was messing around and the dart slipped out of his hand, flying straight into the back of my head! It **stuck** there for a minute (miraculously it didn't hurt) as I turned to see the horrified looks on everyone's faces. As if I wasn't embarrassed enough, I had to get a **tetanus** shot that night! No one has forgotten my birthday crisis."

brotherly love

" I was hanging out with my friends, and we met up with this group of guys we usually hang out with, including the guy I really like. Everything was going well with my crush—until this other group of girls came up to "**our**" guys. All of my friends were pissed, and I was really **annoyed** because this one girl went right up to my crush! So I went to her and said, "*Excuse* me!" She turned around and said, "*What?!*" Then I was like, "*What* are you doing?" and she said, "I'm talking to my **brother**!" Oops. "

totally phone-y

" So my friend and I were at the park, and these guys were looking at us. Finally they came over to talk. We **fake-flirted** with them for a while and said we had to go. We thought we'd be **smart** and give them our fake "rejection" **numbers.** Later, though, we changed our minds about the guys and tried to **call** them up. It turns out they'd given *us* fake numbers too. "

nailed it

"My friends and I were getting acrylic nails for the first time. After the guy finished, he said, "**Lick** it." I couldn't really understand his accent—so I asked, "Lick it?" and he nodded. I licked my **nail**—assuming it was like a special technique used for acrylics or something. The polish was still wet so it got all smeared and **clumped** up. He looked at me like I was crazy but then took off the polish and fixed it as if nothing happened. Then I realized he had been asking if I **liked** it.

drop everything

" I was waiting for the bus one **Saturday,** wearing my new black beret because it had just snowed. Right as the bus came, I felt **something** hit my hat, but I figured it was just snow from the tree. I went through my **whole** day running errands— and then met up with my friend. She told me I had a huge splatter of **white** bird droppings all over my black hat! "

friends

crash and burn

"One night my girlfriends and I decided to go to a **party**. We wore high heels, tight shirts, did our hair—the whole nine yards. We pulled up to the house where the party was **supposed** to be, went in, and made our way all the way to the back. We didn't see any familiar faces, so we walked back toward the front of the house, and I suddenly realized that the **reason** I didn't recognize anyone was because we were in the wrong place! We had crashed someone else's party!**"**

dust buster

" Things were going fine with the little **girl** that my friend and I were babysitting until she became **hyper** and knocked over a vase. I picked up the pieces and vacuumed the **mess,** not realizing that it was her grandfather's remains. **"**

towel dry

"I was at my friend's house, and I went to use the bathroom. I really had to go, so I hadn't even realized there wasn't any **toilet** paper before I sat down. I looked around her bathroom for some after I was done, but there wasn't any in there. I had no choice but to wipe my butt with her **towel.** I slept over that night and felt awful when my friend used that same towel to wrap her **hair** up after her shower the next morning."

lost in translation

" Living in Milan for four years **still** hasn't made me an expert in Italian. Just recently, my friend and I were in a **bakery** and we wanted to know if the bread was made with preservatives. So I used the word *preservativi*. My face turned a bright shade of **red** when I was corrected. *Conservanti* means preservatives. What I'd asked was if the bread had **condoms.** "

friends
oh, brother

"One night I called my best friend Paul to chat, and when he answered, I immediately started talking about how **hot** his brother looked that day. I was talking about how cute his **butt** looked in his jeans. I was like, "Dude, you *need* to hook me up with him—are you listening?" He said, "Paul's not here right now." *I was talking to his hot brother!* I couldn't believe it—they sounded **exactly** the same! I was so embarrassed that I just hung up really fast and then didn't dare call Paul's house for at least the next month."

unhap-pee day

"My friends from my old school met up, and we were doing **impressions** of crazy people we knew. I had to go to the bathroom, but I just held it. But the story was so funny, I peed all over myself, on the chair, and on the **floor**! Then, on the drive home, my friend decided she had to stop at CVS. I was totally **soaked,** waiting in the parking lot, and up drove the guy I was seeing! He came over and my friends started laughing, saying things like, "We're hap-pee to see you!" He drove off, and I probably heard from him once after that."

flash dance

" While I was moshing at a Marilyn Manson/Hole concert, a friend lifted me up to crowd-surf. My shirt started **tearing** as I was being passed along, exposing my bra. I guess a photographer was there, because my picture—with an article about how hard-core music was **corrupting** today's teens—made the arts and entertainment page of the local **paper.** Let's just say my dad wasn't too happy! "

friends

batting practice

" My best friend had a candy-filled pinata at her party. I planned to impress my crush by **whacking** the pinata really hard. My friends spun me around 15 times and I was off-balance, but I finally located the **piñata** to my left. I swung with all my might, felt the bat make contact but then heard a **scream.** As I took off the blindfold, I thought I'd see candy strewn all over the floor, and instead I found some girl **kneeled** over in pain. I felt so bad! "

spotting a fake

" My friend Julie got breast implants three **weeks** ago, and we decided catch up about it all. I picked her up, and while we were at a light she wanted me to check out her boob job, so I **reached** over to feel one of her breasts. Just at that moment, a truck full of teenage guys pulled up next to us, rolled down their window and yelled, "Lesbian action!" They were all whistling and hooting at us. So of course when the **light** turned green, I peeled out of there! "

dr. oh no!

"I took a crowded bus to my gynecologist's appointment. I started **chatting** with the woman sitting next to me, and she asked me where I was **headed.** I told her, she nodded, and we continued our conversation. When my stop came, the bus was so **packed** that I was having trouble getting off. She shouted, "C'mon, people, let the young lady get to her **gynecologist** on time!" The passengers parted, and I slunk off the bus."

sweet spot

" I was in one of those candy shops that sells goodies by the pound. While deciding which candy to buy, I marveled at this really cool dispenser. **Curious,** I pressed my hand against the tube to see exactly how the candy comes out. Suddenly these candies were **pouring** out, covering my feet and the floor. Everyone in the store turned around and **stared.** My friends walked away, pretending they didn't know me. The cashier walked over and politely asked me to leave the store. "

friends

door prize

"My friends and I saw a handicapped sign by a door, so we figured it was one of those **electronic** doors. When I walked up to the door, nothing happened—so I started **swaying** back and forth. These two little ol ladies were totally staring at me. I was like, "There must be something wrong. I can't figure out how to get this door to **open**!" One of the ladies came over and said, "Well, you just have to push it, dear." Turns out that it **wasn't** an automatic door after all.

friends

between the lines

" I was at the fair with my friends and saw this really cool **ride.** There wasn't a line, so I ran right in. The man working there came over—and started pointing and **yelling** at me to get out. I hurried to out of there, but I didn't know why. Outside the ride, my friend told me I had waltzed in through the **exit**—and there was a huge line of people waiting to get in! "

pet peeved

" My neighbor has this cute dog named Blackie. One day, as I stepped out my front door, I could see him coming toward me, so I **yelled** "Hey, Blackie!" Right as I said it, I noticed an African-American man passing my house on the **sidewalk**— and he thought I was talking to *him*! He looked at me like I was a total **freak.** "

shout it out

"At a 98° **concert**, a DJ was getting the crowd all psyched before the show. He asked the girls in the audience to scream, and the response was **deafening.** Then he said, "Now I know there are some guys here... let me hear all the guys **scream**!" So I belted out, "Right here!" Too bad I was the only guy in the entire place to yell."

bunny blooper

" One day, my family's hunting dog came home with the neighbors' kids rabbit, **dead,** in his mouth. I didn't want to tell the kids what happened, so my friend and I cleaned off the **bunny** and snuck it back into the cage. Later, the kids saw the rabbit and started screaming. My friend and I asked what was wrong, but we ended up being **shocked** when the older girl cried out, "We buried our dead bunny three days ago, and now he's **back** in the cage!" Guess our hunting dog was more of a digging dog. "

whiz kid

" When I was **camping** with my friends in the woods, I woke up in the middle of the night to go to the bathroom. I fumbled my way in the dark toward what I **thought** was an empty spot on the ground. I dropped my PJ's and crouched, only to find myself squatting next to this random guy's **head**! It startled me so much that I leaked on my legs and his sleeping bag. "

peek-a-boob

" My friends and I went to a theme park and headed straight to this **crazy** loop roller coaster, where they snap pictures of passengers on the ride. It was the best! That is, until I got off and saw a group **laughing** hysterically near the booth where the pictures are displayed. I walked over to check out what was so funny. In one of the pictures, there was a girl whose shirt had flown up as she rode through a loop. She was basically caught **flashing** everyone! I started to giggle too, until I realized that the girl in the picture was **me**! "

pregnant pause

"One night while I was working behind the counter of the smoothie shop, a round-bellied **woman** walked in. The drink she asked for contained an ingredient that my **manager** told me was bad for pregnant women, so being the ever-so-helpful employee that I am, I **warned** her about the potential danger. She paused, gave me an annoyed look and told me that she was **not** with child. Oops!"

friends

blue moon

"At a Halloween party, my friends and I decided to play Truth or Dare. We were **dared** to moon the next car that passed by. As the next car approached, we dropped our pants for a long, shocking moon. The car **slammed** on its brakes and started to reverse! We ran frantically into the house. Seconds later the doorbell rang—the driver was our **principal**! After a long talk with my mom, we had enough embarrassment to last the entire year—which was about how long I was grounded."

friends

remote outta control

" After finally putting the neighbors' **kids** to bed, my friend and I decided to watch TV but couldn't figure out how to change the **channel** on the family's weird digital-cable system. While fiddling with the remote, I accidentally ordered a **porn** flick! Needless to say, we didn't get hired to baby-sit there again. "

shake down

"Me and my best friends got **bored** sitting around at home, so we went to our local doughnut shop. We ordered Oreo milkshakes and started talking and **flirting** with the hot guy behind the counter while he made them for us. He handed them over, and we ran to the outside chairs to talk about how cute he was. The next thing we know, the guy is right there at our table! I was really excited that he'd **followed** us, until he said, "Um, you didn't pay?" It was so humiliating."

rock 'n' roll

"I was at a concert with my friends, and I had to go to the bathroom. I went into a portable **toilet** and told my friends to wait for me outside. There was a group of guys nearby play-fighting, and suddenly one of them threw another against the out-house stall that I was in. It started to **shake** and then it just tumbled over—with me inside! Let's just say it was totally a **gross** experience."

friends

broken record

"During the Sno-Core '99 tour, I was incredibly psyched to see Everclear, because I was **majorly** into their bassist, Craig Montoya. I was in the front row yelling, "I **love** you, Craig Montoya!" over and over again. Finally the lead singer, Art Alexakis, looked straight at me and said, "Would you **please** stop screaming our bass player's name?""

friends

square in a circle

" I was at a teen club where people "rave," which is when one person dances in the **middle** of a circle while everyone else watches. (I don't know how to do it.) I was **danc-ing** with this hot guy when he pushed me into the middle of the circle. I was in shock so I just **froze.** Everyone started yelling at me to **move** until someone finally pushed me out of the circle. That hot guy didn't even look at me for the rest of the night and I've never ever gone back to the club! "

disappearing act

"My friends and I were at a costume party. After consuming too much punch, I took a bathroom break. I removed my huge witch robe and hung it outside (I was wearing a totally **see-thru** leotard underneath). When I came out, my costume was gone! Everyone was in the living room telling **ghost** stories, so I tried to sneak up the stairs to get some clothes. As I passed through the hall, my friend shined a **flashlight** on me and said, "Ooh! Now *that's* scary!" Everyone laughed. I wanted desperately to melt into the floor."

friends

total exposé

" My friend's sister had opened a clothing **boutique** in a ritzy town and she was putting together a fashion show. One of the models dropped out last minute and since I'm **tall,** my friend asked if I would model in the runway show. I was **totally** flattered so of course I said yes. The night of the show, I felt like a **star.** First of all, the place was really fancy and the off the shoulder dress I had to model was at least $500! So I totally strutted my stuff like a **supermodel** but when I got backstage from the runway I realized my dress had fallen below my chest on one side, **exposing** my bra the whole time. Needless to say that was the end of my big modeling career and my friend got to know me better than he ever could have wanted! "

Two more reasons that modeling career...

...never quite took off.

"Her ring dropped right into my crack!"

see page 160

school

Nothing like being in ~~front~~ of an audience when you just want to **evaporate**.

through the cracks

"In class one day, I felt something hard and cold fall down the back of my **pants.** The girl behind me was messing around with her ring, and it dropped right into my **crack**! She looked around and asked me if it was under my desk. So I pretended to look for it—because there was no **way** I was going to dig it out of my pants in the middle of class. When nobody was looking, I took it out of my pants and **discreetly** dropped it nearby so she'd find it on her own."

standing oh!

"

At the "Goodbye Assembly" for **seniors,** I received an award in front of the entire student body, faculty, and parents. The guy introducing me was pretty **nervous.** Instead of saying, "She has had a lot of success in her high school career,' what came out was, "She has had a lot of **sex** in her high school career." The entire gym started laughing, and I got a **huge** stand ing ovation from all the guys in my class. I was mortified— especially because I'm totally not like that!

"

pickup game

"I had a crush on this basketball player in college. He was a friend of a friend, and I worked up the **nerve** to leave him a message to wish him good luck in the next game. My first three attempts at leaving the perfect **message** didn't go well, so in the middle I would hang up, thinking that it was deleted because I didn't hit the # key to send it. The **fourth** time was the charm, and I was really proud of myself—until a few days later when my friend called to ask me why I had left his friend four crazy messages! Needless to say, the guy never bothered to call me back."

two faced

"I looked at my math quiz and saw that I only had the **first** page. So I raised my hand and said I **needed** the last part of the test. The teacher was like, "Sweetie, it's double-**sided**!" The whole class was laughing!"

seeing double

"I was so excited about going to a new school that I chose my first day outfit **three** weeks before school started. It was perfect: a cute shirt and a **matching** skirt. But when I went to my first class, my English teacher, Mrs. Dunn, was wearing the **exact** same shirt-and-skirt set! Suddenly my new name was Mrs. Dunn.
I was **so** bummed."

school

american idle

" I'm a cheerleader, and at one of our home matches, the coach randomly asked me if I would **sing** the national anthem. I wasn't going to turn him down, but I had no advance warning and didn't even have time to practice! They announced me and I stepped up to the mic. But then I completely **froze**! So I just began to say the pledge of allegiance instead. Everyone in the gym went **along** with it, but the coach hasn't asked me to sing since! "

mortifying period

"I had horrible **cramps** and I asked the school nurse for a note to get out of gym, which is my first class of the day. Not wanting to be **nosy,** I didn't read the note; I just dropped it off for my gym teacher, who also happened to be my basketball coach—and a **man.** A few minutes later he came up to me and gave me a speech on how **great** it was that I had become a woman!"

rocket scientist

"I was in this really hard physics class, and as we were getting ready for a big exam, I was feeling very **stressed** out. My teacher was filling the board with all sorts of obscure symbols and numbers, deltas, **lambdas,** and heaven knows what else. I was trying to keep up, writing everything in my notebook and getting really **confused.** Finally I raised my hand and asked, "What does "**if**" stand for?" Everyone in the class started to laugh. "If, Allie," my teacher said. "If stands for the word if."

to bee or not to bee

"Track team tryouts can be really intense. I was doing fine at mine until I thought I saw a bee **buzzing** around me—I lost my concentration and started screaming hysterically. I ran over to the coach—I was afraid of getting stung and having an **allergic** reaction. Observing my theatrics, the coach said, "I've never seen anyone get so worked up over a **fly.**" I was embarrassed when I realized my insect-classification error."

a real trooper

"My father drove me to school on my first day as a mid-year transfer student. Dad is a state trooper, so of course he was fully **uniformed** when he dropped me off. When I walked into the school all eyes were on me. Later that day, I **overheard** some kids talking about me. One **guy** said he heard I was a trouble-maker who had to be **escorted** to school every day. I thought I would **die**. I never asked my father to bring me to school again."

permanent record

"

During one detention in junior high, I had to write something on an **overhead** projector when the teacher stepped out. I picked up a **marker,** and—just to be funny—wrote a swear word. I tried to wipe it off—then I realized I'd selected a **permanent** marker, not an erasable one! I flipped and started scribbling over the word just as the teacher returned. Phew: He didn't see it, but I got **yelled** at for choosing the wrong pen.

"

athlete's foot

" I was running **late** after gym class, and had to get to math. I didn't have time to change out of my sneakers, and I wasn't wearing any socks, so my feet were all **sweaty.** I have a crush on the guy who sits in front of me and as our teacher started going over our homework, I put my feet on the bottom bar of his **chair.** The hot guy started sniffing and after a few minutes, he realized the smell was from underneath his seat! He blurted out, "Your feet are making me **nauseous**!" *Everyone* in class heard! "

letting go

"

In gym we had a guest teacher come teach us yoga for a week. Well, the first day while she was showing us the downward dog pose, she explained how yoga can relax our bodies. Then, two seconds later, I let out the biggest fart. I was so embarrassed, and to make things worse, the teacher was mad because none of the girls could relax anymore because they were all laughing so hard. I guess yoga does relax your body... maybe a little too much!

"

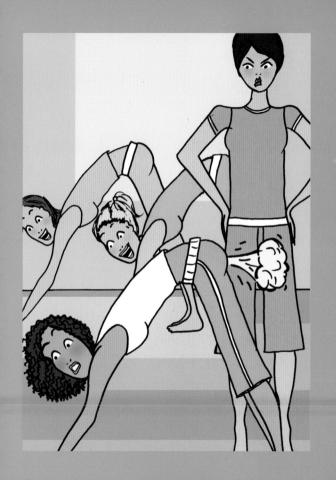

school

thin ice

"My synchronized skating team was at practice, and there were some hot hockey guys **watching** up in the stands. Me and one of my teammates were the **closest** to them, so of course we weren't focusing on what our coach was **saying**! Then, all of a sudden, we heard our coach yell, "Will you stop looking at those guys in the bleachers and pay attention?" We saw the guys **laugh,** and then leave!"

early bird

"At my old school, we had eight periods in the day, but in my new one, there are nine. After eighth period, I **forgot** we had another, so I walked out. I was in the parking lot before I remembered that school **wasn't** finished! I tried to get in the building, but the door was locked. I kept trying to find an **open** door, while all the older kids were yelling, "Hey, that girl is skipping school!" Finally I got in, but to make it worse, my **teacher** wouldn't let me in until I explained to my whole class why I was late."

lowlight

"

I was studying at the library during lunch because I had a huge calculus test next period. I put my hand in my backpack to get a **highlighter** and grabbed something plastic. As I started to highlight, I realized that I had grabbed a plastic-applicator **tampon**! It was out of its wrapper because it had been in my bag for so long. I looked to see if anyone noticed and saw a **tour** of teachers from another school who were checking out our new library. They must have thought that I was nuts!

"

hot pockets

"I was **strolling** down the hall when I noticed this gorgeous guy. I slowed down so I could follow him and get a good view of his, um, back **pockets** (I know, I'm bad). I guess I was concentrating too heavily on his rear, because when he suddenly **stopped,** I kept going—straight into him! My head collided with his shoulder blades and he reeled from the **impact.** I turned the other way and swiftly **retreated** down the hall—before he could send a mean look my way."

school

period drama

"I had finally worked up the nerve to talk to the guy I had a **crush** on, and I wanted to compliment him on a cool history project he'd done about the Egyptian pyramids. But when I actually got up to him, I was so **nervous** that I slipped on my words and ended up saying, "I like the project you did on **periods.**" To make things worse, he yelled "Periods?! I didn't do a project on periods!" Needless to say, we never got together."

sour notes

"Last Valentine's Day, I was sitting in **band** class when the guy next to me said he was going to throw up on me. I didn't worry about it because he disliked me, and I thought he was just being a jerk. Then, all of a **sudden,** he **spewed** all over me! Some had gotten on my instrument too, so when I picked it up, I got even more on me! I started to **freak out,** and went to the bathroom. On my way out, I walked past my ex-boyfriend. I still had feelings for him, and there he was, **laughing** at me—it was the worst Valentine's Day!"

fly girl

"I had completely forgotten it was picture day and arrived at school in a blah outfit with **totally** flat hair. I wasn't happy about being photographed, but when I got the **pictures** back a week later, I saw there was a **fly** sitting on my shoulder— that was even grosser than my hair!"

teacher's fret

> It was the first day of my freshman year at college, and I was taking an English tutorial that was being taught by a teacher's **assistant**. After 10 minutes had passed and the TA still hadn't shown up, I stood up and went on and on about how unprofessional it was for him to be late. When I had finished **ranting** and raving, the guy who was sitting in front of me walked to the front of the classroom—and introduced **himself** as our TA for the semester.

school

band geek

"I was in class with this guy I have a crush on, when I noticed his **book** had lots of stickers all over it. He saw me **staring** and asked if I had ever heard of any of those **bands** before. I pointed at this big, shiny sticker that said Vans on it and was like, "Yeah, I've heard of them!" He gave me this totally weird look and said, "Uh, Vans are **sneakers...**" Thank goodness the bell rang right then to save me from any more self-humiliation. I felt like a total moron."

toeing the line

" I was playing **soccer** and suddenly the arch of my left foot started to hurt and I couldn't run anymore. So, I went up to the coach and told him I needed to sit out because I had a **camel toe** and it hurt too bad to play. He was like, "Okay, a camel toe?—Um, sure, come sit down." It was only later, after I got home, that I realized I'd totally used the **wrong** term—I had a charley horse, definitely not a camel toe! "

poetic justice

" For the first day of English class, I was at home with the **flu.** I called up a friend who was in my class to see what I missed. He said we had to write a **poem** about why we had chosen that particular course. The following day, when the teacher asked for someone to read their homework **out loud,** I volunteered. I was reciting my poem (which was good!) when I realized the whole class was **snickering.** Turns out my friend was playing a joke on me—the poem wasn't the real assignment. "

follow the leader

"I was walking down the hall, toward the **bathroom,** and I saw my professor in front of me. He turned to the left, and without thinking I followed him—into the **wrong** bathroom! He didn't see me at first but went to a urinal and started to **unzip** his pants just as I realized where I was. I froze and our eyes met in the mirror. I **yelled,** "Oh my God!" and just ran out. I was so traumatized that I didn't go to class for a **week,** hoping he would forget my face and think I was someone else."

school

dummy up

"One day in first-aid class, our teacher told us that we'd have to be extra **mature** for the lesson and we had no idea why. She went on to tell us that if there was an unconscious **man** with a spinal injury, we should check for (I swear!) an erect penis! She then asked me to **demonstrate** how I would go about feeling for an erection. I have no idea how many colors my face turned as I groped around the dummy's **crotch,** but I *do* know that the rest of the class was hysterically laughing the whole time!"

school outing

"A guest speaker in health class asked us to write down **anonymous** questions. All my life I'd wondered whether a woman pees **from** her clitoris, so I asked about it on the card. The good thing was he read my **question** to the class; the bad thing was I'd actually written my name on it, and he read that **aloud,** too! Everyone cracked up, but it'll take **forever** to live it down."

199

flower show

"Ever the egomaniac, I sent a whole bunch of flowers to myself on my birthday, in the hopes of **looking** like I had a secret admirer. But when the **roses** arrived at school, the teacher read the card to the whole class: The **stupid** florist had written down my name as both the giver and receiver."

spitting image

"

While on my school's annual outing to the zoo, I was cracking people up by imitating some **chimps** who were **grooming** each other. Suddenly one of them got mad, swung toward the fence and spit a huge yellow **goober** all over me. Blech! I freaked out and started to **cry,** but all my classmates were howling! I felt like I was an extra on *Animal Planet*.

"

school

ups and downs

"One year, my high school music department had a field trip to Six Flags Great Adventure for all the kids in band, orchestra, and chorus. I'm a total roller coaster **addict** so I was extra excited. Plus, it was the first time we were spending any time with our teachers outside of school, so that added a **funny** layer as well. Anyway, one of the teachers was this totally **conservative** guy so it was hilarious to see him wearing shorts instead of his usual shirt and tie! (Think super **pasty** legs!) I decided it would be funny if I snuck up behind him to unfasten his **Velcro** back pockets as a joke. I didn't realize they'd be so stiff so I ended up having to **yank** them really hard and...well, let's just say we all learned that he wears tighty **whities**!"

Me, before I started reading Seventeen.

My brain is in here somewhere...

"I ended up
flashing 35 coed
cross-country
teams!"

see page 214

fashion

Even the best-dressed intentions can have humiliating consequences.

fashion
sole searching

"I was shoe shopping with friends and we were waiting for the guy to bring me a pair of **cute** heels. While I was sitting, I saw these perfect **shoes** next to my chair. I decided to try them on and started walking around in them. After about two minutes, a woman came up to me and said, "Those are **my** shoes!" I didn't understand at first, but then it hit me—she'd left her shoes behind while she tried on another pair! She got really **annoyed** with me about the whole thing—and I felt so dumb!"

panty raid

"I went over to my boyfriend's house after school one day, and I **needed** to go **number two** really bad! So I told him I was going to the kitchen, but I really went to the bathroom. When I got to the bathroom I looked at my panties—and saw a huge poop stain. I panicked and **threw** them out the window so I wouldn't smell. Later when my boyfriend walked me home he saw them and said, "There are some **nasty** people in the world!""

miss understood

"My friends and I were buying some little **tops** and underwear. There was this cute guy at the register **flirting** with us while he rang up my stuff. At one point, he looked at me and said, "Can I have **y'all's** phone numbers?" and I went, "Well, you can have one of theirs, but you're not getting mine 'cause I have a boyfriend!" He said he **wasn't** asking for himself—that it was store protocol to put the number in the computer! I was just like, "**Oh**"—but I was obviously so embarrassed!"

flirting with disaster

"So I went to this big party in Philly for my older cousin's birthday. I had been sitting and talking for almost two hours with this really **hot** guy I'd just met. He kept telling me how cute my **outfit** was and wanted to know where I got my vintage Green Day T-shirt. Finally, near the end of the night, I got up enough nerve to go in for a **kiss.** But just as I was about to, he freaked out, held me back—and told me that he was gay! It was **really** awkward!"

fashion

comic strip

" Last season one of our cross-country **races** took place on a really rainy day, and afterward my teammates and I decided to go **mud** sliding. But we didn't want to get our clothes all dirty, so we stripped down to **sports bras** and bun huggers (kind of like swimming suit bottoms). Well, I was **talking** to some friends while pulling off my top, and I got so distracted that somehow I took my bra off too! I ended up **flashing** 35 coed cross-country teams! "

fashion

sarong song

" It was the first day of spring, and I wanted to show my "carefree" **spirit** by wearing my new blue sarong that my dad got me on a trip to Bali. I was walking down the hall feeling excited about my **cute** outfit, when this guy behind me accidentally stepped on my sarong, **pulling** the whole thing down to reveal my flesh-colored **thong**! But that's not the worst of it: The guy didn't realize it and kept walking—with it caught in his sneaker! I had to run after him half-naked to get my sarong back! **"**

wrong note

" I had a crush on the guitarist from a local band. I knew him through a mutual friend, who **invited** me to go to one of their concerts. I got there early to be at the front. My friend had **told** me that my crush liked girls who like to have fun and who aren't **shy.** I used this information, and during one of their songs, I **jumped** up on the stage! But as soon as I got up there, my super-slinky halter top got **caught** on the cage platform, ripped, and then fell to my waist! He looked at me like I was an idiot. P.S. I don't take my friend's advice anymore! "

get a grip

> I'm walking through Old Navy, and I'm wearing these really fun, heeled flip-flops. I don't know if the floor was wet, but I slip horribly and start to fall. On my way down, I reached out and **grabbed** whatever I could to keep myself from hitting the floor. And I grabbed this woman's **breast**! Like full on *grabbed* it! If it was a horn, it would have *honked*. She freaks out and starts screaming at me—all I could do was just stand there and **apologize** over and over.

fashion

maxi-mum security

"

I was with my best friend at SeaWorld, and I'd just gotten my **period** the day before. I wanted to be able to just have **fun,** so I *jammed* my bag with pads to make sure I would be totally **safe** all day. Of course, it was just my luck that with all the new **security** regulations my purse would have to be checked—by a really cute guy! I was totally mortified!

"

fashion

dive-bombed

"This hot guy Ryan was a lifeguard at the **pool,** so I wore my bright-pink bikini there. I wanted to show off my diving skills, but I was nervous my bathing suit might come **off.** I went up to the diving board though and dove—but my top came off! I stayed underwater trying to tie it on, and Ryan thought I was **drowning**! He dove in and pulled me, **topless,** up to the side of the pool! I was soembarrassed, I just grabbed my top and ran!"

sticky situation

"I had a major crush on my friend's brother, so one day when I was over at her house I did a little **snooping.** I went into her brother's room and saw a **picture** of him and his girlfriend. When I went to pick up the picture to look at it, my chewing gum fell into his **underwear** drawer! Obviously I was freaking, trying to find it. I thought I felt the gum stuck in a pair of his **boxers,** so I picked them up and was looking in them—when his mom walked in! I acted like I was trying to find something, but she must think I'm a total sicko!"

overexposed

"Shopping for bras and undies became a revealing experience for my friend and I. We were in different dressing rooms and briefly **stepped** out to see each other's choices. But when we tried to reenter our stalls, we found we'd both been **locked** out! Looking for someone who could let us back in was the **longest** two minutes of my life."

fashion

neck lace

"I was in the middle of changing after **gym** class when a friend called me over for a quick chat. I threw on a sweatshirt and went over to speak with her—and forgot that my **bra** was around my neck. It wasn't until the next period that I noticed the bra. I was hoping that somehow my **faux pas** had gone undetected, but no such luck. The rest of the day everyone was asking where my "sporty **necklace**" was."

yule-tide

" Our family always comes over for Christmas, and this year my new **boyfriend** came. I had my period, but I was wearing a thin pad since it was light. Big mistake! I was sitting on our **white** carpet and as I stood up, my little cousin screamed, "Ew, gross!" and pointed to a **huge** blood stain! I ran to the bathroom, and when I got back, everyone was discussing the best way to get the stain out of the carpet. I guess it will be a long time before **anyone** lets me forget about that! "

sticker shock

" For my birthday I got a pair of black **jeans.** They looked so cool, I decided to wear them to school the next day. When I got up in the morning, I **excitedly** threw on my jeans and a blue T-shirt. All morning I walked through the halls psyched about my hot **outfit.** Then at lunch a friend totally burst my fashion bubble by casually pointing out that the size and style stickers were still on the back of my jean leg! "

diaper splash

"After my friends and I went swimming in the ocean, we noticed white cotton threads and shreds of clear plastic **clinging** to our hair and our swimsuits. We tried combing and rinsing the stuff out, but nothing worked for several **gross** days and the strings clung to our swimsuits like tape. By then, we'd figured out that the sticky **strands** were the vile remains of a waterlogged, disintegrated diaper."

fashion
bummed out

"

I got my hair done on prom day, but the appointment ran long. I called my boyfriend to tell him I was running **behind.** I hurried as fast as I could—miraculously, I was all set by the time he came. We took **pictures** in my front yard. As we were getting ready to finally leave, one of my boyfriend's **relatives** tapped me on the shoulder and whispered that I'd forgotten to fasten all the buttons in the back of the dress, and my **butt** was showing the whole time!

"

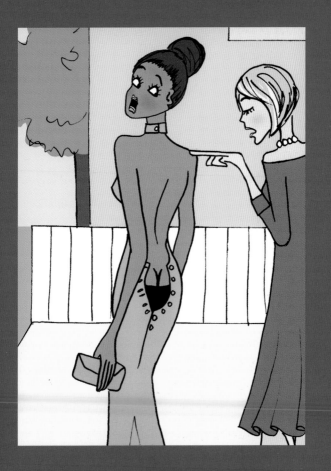

fashion

glowing review

" On the night my friends and I went bowling, the alley was lit with black lights, and all of our white clothing **glowed** in the dark. At this one point, this **cute** bunch of boys asked to take a picture of us, so we smiled and **posed** for them. Later on, we realized why the guys were so interested—our white **panties** were shining through our skirts! We made for the door and never went back. **"**

tight squeeze

"

On the hunt for a miniskirt, I finally found a perfect little leopard-print number. When the small—my usual size—didn't come close to **fitting,** I selected the next one up, but it was also too snug. I put on every size, but even the extra large was too **tiny.** When I explained my problem to the saleslady, she smiled and told me that I had been trying to **squeeze** my butt into a tube top. Oops!

"

sweating it out

"After my teacher caught me chewing gum in class, I was told to do a half-hour of **detention** later in the week. Since I knew my crush would be there, I got really **dressed** up on that day. I strolled into detention and—irony alert—sat down on some gum. I had to go to the nurse's office to **borrow** a pair of disgusting sweat-pants and wear them the entire time."

fashion

all caught up

"I went to my junior prom with a very chivalrous senior, who pulled out and pushed in my **chair** for me when I sat down for dinner. What I didn't know was that the bottom of my **long** dress had gotten caught under the legs of my chair. Later, when I excused myself to go to the bathroom, I stood up but my dress **stayed** down! I was so glad I'd decided to wear a strapless bra rather than go bra-less, which was my original plan. Ugh!"

fashion

stringing him along

" One day my crush and I were walking along the boardwalk near the **restaurant** where we worked. I was excited to spend some time with him—alone. We decided to get ice cream and found a place to sit. Well, I **forgot** that I had my period, and as we sat down to eat, he noticed my **tampon** string hanging out of my very short shorts. To make matters worse, he **tugged** on it, asking, "Hey, what's this?" Thankfully he truly didn't have a clue what it was! "

in a flash

"

At a summer camp one day my friend and I wanted to go for a quick swim. I **threw** on my bikini and ran to meet her at the pool. I glanced down as I was about to dive and saw that I'd put the bottoms on the **wrong** way. The skinnier strap that was **supposed** to be at my hip was in my *crotch,* and I was showing **way** more than I'd intended!

"

fashion

cast away

> My new bathing suit seemed perfect: The push-up-style stuffing made my chest look huge. But when I went for a swim at the beach, everyone started **staring** at me. I thought they were envious of my great backstroke, but then I looked down at the water and spotted one of my "breasts" **floating** beside me. Oh, my heavens! I turned beet-red, grabbed my pad, and **swam** for cover.

fashion

read it 'n' weep

" I was shopping with friends when we spotted this **awesome** store. There was a huge sign in the window that said WE'LL PUT A MESSAGE ON A T-SHIRT FOR $7. We all decided to get our **crushes** names printed on. I asked the salesperson to put Dan (the name of my crush) on my shirt in huge letters, and then we all put on our **tees.** When we left the store, guess who was standing there looking surprised? Yup—Dan! He laughed and said, "Nice shirt!" "

fall girl

"
I was a bridesmaid in a wedding and had to make a big entrance with one of the cute groomsmen. He escorted me onto the recently **waxed** floor, but when he gallantly pulled me toward him to start **dancing,** I slipped in my brand-new shoes and wiped out in front of 150 people. Everyone **gasped,** but when I got up, they all started clapping. I blushed for an hour.
"

walk of shame

"I was sitting at a table in the cafeteria, **admiring** my longtime crush from across the room. Just to impress him, I'd worn a **miniskirt** and a little tee that day, and I planned to walk by him so he could drool over me. As I started **strutting** my stuff across the room, I noticed tons of kids checking me out. Finally a girl came up and said, "You have an onion ring with **ketchup** stuck to the back of your skirt!" Not quite the impression I was going for."

indecent exposure

"I wanted to feel extra-sexy on prom night, so I wore a black garter belt and thigh-high **stockings** under my dress. When I started dancing, I realized I'd have to hold my puffy dress to keep from tripping on it. I was on the floor, **swinging** my skirt around when the principal **called** me out. She announced at the top of her lungs that everyone could **see** my "inappropriate underwear!" It was all I heard about for the rest of the night."

fashion

bottoms up

" While sporting my cheerleading skirt in class, I realized I wasn't wearing my flash **panties**—special briefs that are similar to bathing-suit bottoms—for the big game! So I called Mom and asked her to drop them off. An hour later, the school secretary **barged** into class, holding up my red **bloomers.** "Is there a Christine here?" she asked. Everyone was gawking. I wanted to crawl into a hole and die. "

fashion

x-ray vision

"

When I first started *CosmoGIRL!* (my job before *Seventeen*), I had bought this **amazing** black dress by Ann Demeulemeester (one of my favorite designers). I was feeling great about myself because I'd never had a **dress** by her even though I'd always coveted her designs. So when Mark Montano, one of our contributors, was being honored at a big awards ceremony, I knew just the dress to wear—I felt like a **goddess.** So of course, I was jumping into every picture—after all, I had my dream job, my dream dress—I was on top of the world. Uh...until I saw some of those **pictures** the next day and realized that my dress was totally **see-through** and my decision to not wear a bra really illustrated that point. Ah yes, another proud moment for my poor parents...

"

The bride of Rubenstein.

What?? He said I looked fat!

index